bite sized

Mexican

First published in 2001 by Hamlyn
an imprint of Octopus Publishing Group Ltd.
2-4 Heron Quays
London E14 4JP

Copyright © 2001 Octopus Publishing Group Ltd.

A CIP catalogue record for this book is available from the British Library

ISBN 0-600-60326-1

Printed and bound in China

10 9 8 7 6 5 4 3 2 1

Notes

Standard level spoon measurements are used in all recipes
1 tablespoon = one 15 ml spoon
1 teaspoon = one 5 ml spoon

Both imperial and metric measurements have been given in all recipes.
Use one set of measurements only and not a mixture of both.

Eggs should be medium unless otherwise stated.

Pepper should be freshly ground black pepper unless otherwise stated.

Fresh herbs should be used unless otherwise stated. If unavailable, use dried
herbs as an alternative but halve the quantities stated.

Ovens should be preheated to the specified temperature - if using a
fan-assisted oven, follow the manufacturer's instructions for adjusting the
time and temperature.

hamlyn

bite-sized
Mexican

contents

Introduction

Just like Mexico and the people who live there, Mexican food is colourful, bright and exciting. With its wafts of aromatic smells heralding rich, savoury flavours, Mexican food grabs the attention of the nostrils, stimulating the taste-buds and the appetite and making it very hard to resist.

The evolution of Mexican cuisine is steeped in history. The Aztec and Mayan population were farmers and fishermen, and lived on a diet of wild game, turkey, fish and shellfish, tropical fruit, chillies and avocados. These tribes cultivated cacao – to produce chocolate – beans, corn, chillies, and many other crops that have become major constituents of the world's food. However, the arrival of the Spanish in 1519 brought sweeping changes to the national cuisine. They brought with them a range of European foods including dairy products and beef, as well as many

exotic ingredients that they had picked up from their colonial trade links across the world. Consequently today's Mexican cuisine is a blend of the original native fare with some European ingredients and cooking methods.

Food is an important element of Mexican culture, with much of the daily routine and tradition revolving around the ritual of the preparation and eating of food. Mexicans have gradually become great snack-eaters, largely because of the meal patterns that have evolved over the years to fit in with daily work routines and the demands of the climate. An early breakfast at dawn, *desayuno*, means that by about eleven or twelve o'clock, a second breakfast, *almuerzo*, is needed, with items such as Ranchero Eggs (see page 28), Refried Beans (see page 63) or perhaps a torta (the Mexican version of a sandwich). Lunch, *comida*, eaten anytime between two and four in the afternoon will be the main

meal of the day and might consist of as many as four courses, including a *sopa seca* (literally 'dry' soup, a dish made of pasta or rice cooked in sauce, see page 70), meat, poultry or fish. This meal is followed by a siesta of some hours. The next meal, *cena*, is not until eight or nine in the evening, and will consist of something quite light, such as Ceviche (marinated fish, see page 68). Because of these long gaps between meals, bite-sized food that can be eaten easily is often necessary to top up energy levels.

Antojitos – little whims or bite-sized nibbles – make up a food category all of their own in Mexico. The well-established street food culture provides a rich fund of dishes that are easy to assemble and eat. Foremost among this type of food are tortilla-based items – quesadillas, tacos, enchiladas, burritos and fajitas – all of which can be filled with a wide range of ingredients in a variety of combinations. It is simple to create these

dishes at home, using whatever ingredients are to hand in your refrigerator, store cupboard or freezer, and they are also a great way of putting leftovers to good use.

As well as these more familiar snacks, you will find less well-known dishes such as Panuchos (see page 47), chicken-stuffed tortillas(see page 58), refried beans and eggs (see page 47) and the delightful deep-fried pastry parcels, Sopaipillas (see page 23). Also included are the essential dips and salsas to accompany the snacks.These dishes also make great party food; many can be prepared in advance and assembled at the last minute, while others are perfect for sharing or as buffet snacks.

So, be adventurous, and allow a touch of spice and a splash of colour into your culinary world with these exciting bite-sized recipes!

glossary

Avocado

Called *ahuacatl* by the Aztecs, avocados grew wild throughout Central America and Mexico as early as AD 900. This fruit has a smooth creamy taste, but was originally considered quite bland by early cultures. Use lemon juice to stop the flesh from discolouring when cut.

Cheese

Although Mexico had no cheese before the Spanish conquest, it has become an essential element of many different dishes. Most Mexican cheese is still made on only a small scale today, and very little is exported, but other cheeses can be substituted where a Mexican cheese is listed in the ingredients. American Monterey Jack, or a mixture of Cheddar and mozzarella, can be used where a recipe requires melting cheese; and good Wensleydale, Lancashire, Cheshire, or Greek feta can be used instead of the Mexican *queso fresca* for scattering over the top of a dish.

Chilli peppers

Mexicans use a wide variety of chillies, not just for their heat but also for their different flavours. There are more than 100 varieties of chilli available, at varying levels of fieriness.

* *Anaheim*: these large green chillies have a mild subtle taste and are often served stuffed with several ingredients.
* *Jalapeño*: a very hot and pungent all-purpose chilli pepper. Great for salsas, dips and pickled hot peppers.
* *Orange Habanero*: these are known for their pleated, lantern shape. Fresh Habaneros have a distinctive aroma, which goes well with sauces, seafood and tropical fruits.
* *Red Habanero*: reported to be the hottest pepper available.
* *Scotch Bonnet*: this smaller, Jamaican version of the Habanero takes its name from its resemblance to a Scotsman's floppy bonnet.
* *Thai*: these chillies are rich with oils that coat the mouth with lasting heat.
* *Tabasco*: used exclusively in the sauce of the same name, Tabasco chillies have a unique, dry/hot smoky taste combined with fiery pungency.

Chorizo sausage

A firm, tasty, cured sausage, with a characteristic orange-red colour from the paprika that is used, along with garlic, for flavouring. Chorizo is best bought in a piece rather that pre-sliced.

Cooking fat

Good, well-flavoured lard – clarified and purified pork fat – is widely used in Mexican cooking. However, because it is often not readily available, nor to everyone's taste, vegetable oil can be substituted, although the dish will lose some of its authenticity. Butter and olive oil are rarely used in Mexican cooking.

Coriander

Also known as cilantro and Chinese parsley, fresh coriander is used raw in large amounts, and gives the essential flavour to a number of Mexican dishes, such as Guacamole (see page 76).

Dried pinto beans

These small beans have a mottled pink exterior and are a favourite in Mexican dishes. They combine well with rice and can often be found in stews.

Tortillas

Similar to pancakes, tortillas are the quintessential edible foodwrap. They form the basis of many of the best known Mexican dishes: tacos, tostados, enchiladas, chimichangas and flautas. Tortillas can be made from wheat or from a specially treated cornmeal, which can be difficult to obtain. They are quite tricky to make, and the corn version really needs a special tortilla press. However, wheat tortillas, in particular, are now readily available in supermarkets. Tortillas are always heated before being eaten. They also freeze well.

nibbles and bites

spicy nachos with cheese

totopos

toasted spiced pumpkin seeds

chilli chips

corn fritters

roast corn on the cob

chilli nachos

grilled chicken wings

mexican puffed fritters

sopaipillas

Serves 4–6 / **Preparation time** 30 minutes /
Cooking time about 25–30 minutes

spicy nachos with cheese

- **2 tablespoons oil**
- **1 onion, chopped**
- **2 garlic cloves, crushed**
- **4 large tomatoes, skinned, deseeded and chopped**
- **2 fresh jalapeño chillies, deseeded and chopped**
- **pinch of dried oregano**
- **pinch of ground cumin**
- **250 g (8 oz) tortilla chips**
- **125 g (4 oz) Cheddar cheese, grated**
- **salt and pepper**

TO GARNISH

- **2 spring onions, cut into strips**
- **1 fresh red chilli, deseeded and cut into strips**

1 To make the chilli sauce, heat the oil in a small saucepan and sauté the onion and garlic until soft and golden, stirring the mixture occasionally.

2 Add the tomatoes, chillies, oregano, cumin and salt and pepper to taste. Bring to the boil, reduce the heat and simmer gently for 15 minutes, or until the chilli sauce is thickened and reduced.

3 Arrange the tortilla chips on a large ovenproof dish or plate and carefully spoon the chilli sauce over the top of them. Sprinkle with the grated Cheddar and cook in a preheated oven, 180°C (350°F), Gas Mark 4, for 10–15 minutes, or until the cheese melts and starts to bubble.

4 Soak the spring onion and chilli strips in very cold water for 5–10 minutes to make them curl. Serve the nachos garnished with the spring onion and chilli strips.

totopos

- **oil, for deep-frying**
- **6 tortillas**
- **2 tablespoons grated Parmesan cheese**
- **chilli powder, to taste**

1 Heat the oil in a deep-fryer to 180°C (350°F) or until a cube of bread browns in 30 seconds.

2 Meanwhile, pile the tortillas on top of each other. Cut the pile into quarters then cut the quarters in half, making 8 wedges from each tortilla.

3 Fry the tortilla wedges in batches, shaking the frying basket frequently, for about 2 minutes, until golden and crisp. Remove each batch and drain on kitchen paper. Keep warm while frying the remaining wedges.

4 While still hot, sprinkle over the Parmesan and chilli powder. Serve warm or cold.

Serves 4 / **Preparation time** 5 minutes / **Cooking time** 15 minutes

toasted spiced pumpkin seeds

- **150 g (5 oz) pumpkin seeds**
- **1 teaspoon salt**
- **½ teaspoon mild chilli powder**
- **½ teaspoon ground cumin**

1 Heat a large, heavy-based frying pan. Add a single layer of pumpkin seeds and heat gently until the seeds start to pop, shaking the pan so the seeds cook evenly.

2 Cover the pan and heat for a further minute until the seeds puff and brown slightly, shaking the pan frequently.

3 Mix together the salt, chilli powder and cumin. Sprinkle some of the mixture over the seeds. Cover the pan again and give a final shake. Tip into a shallow dish to cool. Repeat with the remaining seeds and salt mixture. Serve cold.

Serves 4 / **Preparation time** 5 minutes, plus cooling / **Cooking time** about 5 minutes

chilli chips

1 Cut each potato into 8 wedges and place in a large bowl. Add the oil, salt and chilli powder and toss until evenly coated. Preheat the oven to 220°C (425°F), Gas Mark 7.

2 Transfer the potatoes to a baking sheet and roast in the preheated oven for 15 minutes. Turn the potatoes and cook for a further 25–30 minutes, until crisp and golden.

3 Cool slightly and serve with soured cream or mayonnaise, garnished with salad leaves.

- **4 large baking potatoes**
- **4–6 tablespoons oil**
- **½ teaspoon salt**
- **1–2 teaspoons chilli powder, to taste**
- **soured cream or mayonnaise, to serve**
- **salad leaves, to garnish**

Tip Use as little or as much chilli powder as you like to coat these oven-roasted potato chips.

Serves 4–6 / **Preparation time** 5 minutes / **Cooking time** about 1 hour

Serves 4 / **Preparation time** 10 minutes / **Cooking time** 10 minutes

corn fritters

- **300 g (10 oz) frozen sweetcorn kernels, thawed**
- **2 garlic cloves, crushed and finely chopped**
- **1 red chilli, deseeded and finely chopped**
- **2 tablespoons finely chopped coriander**
- **150 g (5 oz) plain flour**
- **1 teaspoon baking powder**
- **2 eggs, beaten**
- **2 tablespoons lime juice**
- **grated rind of 2 limes**
- **oil, for deep-frying**
- **coriander leaves, to garnish**

TO SERVE
- **Tomato Sauce (see page 72)**
- **small, crisp lettuce leaves**

1 In a bowl, beat together the corn, garlic, chilli, coriander, flour, baking powder, eggs, lime juice and rind.

2 In a deep, wide saucepan, heat 5 cm (2 inches) of oil to 180–190°C (350–375°F) or until a cube of bread browns in 30 seconds. Add spoonfuls of the corn mixture in batches and fry for 2–3 minutes. Drain on kitchen paper. Put a warm fritter in each lettuce leaf and spear with a cocktail stick. Trickle over a little tomato sauce and garnish with coriander leaves.

roast corn on the cob

- **4 corn on the cob with the husks**
- **75 g (3 oz) butter**
- **2 garlic cloves, crushed**
- **2 limes, quartered**
- **salt and pepper**

1 Pull the husks away from the corn and remove the silky threads, then soak the husks in cold water for 30–60 minutes. Shake off excess water.

2 Meanwhile, gently heat the butter and garlic in a small saucepan until the butter is sizzling, then remove the pan from the heat.

3 Brush some of the garlic butter liberally over the cobs and fold the husks back into place. Roast in a preheated oven, 220°C (425°F), Gas Mark 7, for 20–30 minutes, until the corn is tender.

4 Fold back the husks, season with salt and pepper to taste and squeeze lime juice over. Serve with the remaining garlic butter.

Serves 4 / **Preparation time** 5 minutes, plus soaking /
Cooking time 20–30 minutes

chilli nachos

1 Place the tortillas on a baking sheet. Sprinkle over the cheese. Cover with the sausage, onion and tomatoes. Add the strips of pimiento or chilli in a criss-cross pattern. Cook in a preheated oven, 200°C (400°F), Gas Mark 6, for about 8 minutes, until the cheese has melted.

2 Cut into 8 wedges to serve as a starter, or into 4 to serve as a snack.

- **2 tortillas, 25–30 cm (10–12 inches) in diameter**
- **500 g (1 lb) Mozzarella cheese, grated**
- **500 g (1 lb) chorizo sausage, skinned and chopped**
- **50 g (2 oz) onion, finely chopped**
- **2 tomatoes, diced**
- **70 g (2¾ oz) can red pimientos or chillies, drained and sliced**

Serves 4 / **Preparation time** 15 minutes / **Cooking time** 8 minutes

Serves 4 / **Preparation time** 15 minutes, plus marinating /
Cooking time 10 minutes

grilled chicken wings

- **2 garlic cloves**
- **1 red chilli, deseeded and chopped**
- **¾ teaspoon ground cinnamon**
- **100 ml (3½ fl oz) fresh orange juice**
- **2 tablespoons tequila**
- **2 tablespoons oil**
- **12 chicken wings**
- **salt**

DIP
- **2 yellow peppers**
- **2 garlic cloves, crushed**
- **50 g (2 oz) soft cheese**
- **milk (optional)**
- **2 tablespoons finely chopped coriander**
- **dash of hot pepper sauce**
- **salt**

1 Crush the garlic with the chilli and a pinch of salt. Mix in the cinnamon, orange juice and tequila. Gradually whisk in the oil until evenly blended.

2 Put the chicken wings in a single layer in a shallow dish. Pour the marinade over and turn the wings to coat them evenly. Cover and chill for 2–3 hours, turning occasionally.

3 Meanwhile, make the dip. Cook the yellow peppers under a preheated hot grill, turning frequently, until charred and blistered. Leave until cool enough to handle, then peel off the skins. Halve the peppers, remove the seeds and chop the flesh. Put into a blender with the garlic and cheese. Process until smooth. Add a little milk, if necessary, to make a dipping consistency. Add the coriander and hot pepper sauce and salt to taste. Chill until required.

4 Remove the chicken wings from the marinade; reserve the marinade. Cook the chicken under a preheated hot grill or on a barbecue, turning and brushing frequently with the reserved marinade, for about 4–5 minutes each side until the skin is golden brown and the juices run clear when the thickest part is tested with a sharp knife. Serve with the dip.

Serves 4–6 / **Preparation time** 15 minutes, plus standing /
Cooking time 30 minutes

mexican puffed fritters

- **250 g (8 oz) plain flour**
- **1 teaspoon baking powder**
- **pinch of salt**
- **1 tablespoon sugar**
- **1 egg, well beaten**
- **2 tablespoons melted butter**
- **125 ml (4 fl oz) milk**
- **oil, for deep-frying**

SYRUP
- **350 ml (12 fl oz) water**
- **4 tablespoons sherry**
- **125 g (4 oz) dark brown sugar**
- **½ cinnamon stick**

1 Sift the flour, baking powder and salt into a large mixing bowl. Stir in the sugar and mix in the egg, butter and enough milk to form a soft, but not too sticky dough.

2 Divide the dough into 8–12 equal pieces. With floured hands, shape each piece into a ball. Cover with a sheet of clingfilm and leave to stand for 30 minutes. Shape into flat cakes and make a shallow depression in the centre of each.

3 Heat the oil to 190°C (375°F) or until a cube of bread browns in 30 seconds. Use a slotted spoon to put the cakes, a few at a time, into the oil and deep-fry them until golden brown and puffy. Drain on kitchen paper.

4 Meanwhile, put all the syrup ingredients into a heavy-based saucepan and bring to the boil over a low heat, stirring. Simmer, stirring occasionally, for 20–30 minutes, until the syrup thickens. Discard the cinnamon stick and serve the syrup with the warm fritters.

Serves 4-6 / **Preparation time** 20 minutes, plus standing /
Cooking time 5-10 minutes

sopaipillas

- 250 g (8 oz) flour
- 1 tablespoon baking powder
- ½ teaspoon salt
- 1 tablespoon oil
- 150-175 ml (5-6 fl oz) lukewarm water
- oil, for deep-frying
- 2 tablespoons honey, warmed with a little ground cinnamon
- fresh pomegranate seeds, to garnish

1   Sift the flour, baking powder and salt into a bowl. Bind with the oil and add enough lukewarm water to form a dough.

2   Knead the dough briefly until it is really smooth. Cover and leave to stand at room temperature for about 20 minutes.

3   Roll out the dough on a lightly floured surface to 5 mm (¼ inch) thick. Cut the dough into 7.5 cm (3 inch) squares.

4   Heat the oil for deep-frying to 200°C (400°F), and deep-fry the pieces of dough, two or three at a time, until they are puffed up and golden. Turn once so that they are evenly coloured on both sides. Drain on kitchen paper. To serve, tear off a corner of each sopaipilla and pour in some honey flavoured with cinnamon. Serve sprinkled with pomegranate seeds.

a bite more

ranchero bread

chicken, bean and avocado rolls

ranchero eggs

eggs with prawns

scrambled eggs with tortilla strips

cauliflower salad

vegetable fajitas

stuffed courgettes

quesadillas

empañadas

meat-stuffed tortillas with salsa

fried beef tortillas

marinated chicken kebabs

chicken enchiladas

ranchero bread

- **150 g (5 oz) cornmeal, plus extra for sprinkling**
- **1 teaspoon salt**
- **½ teaspoon bicarbonate of soda**
- **250 ml (8 fl oz) milk**
- **2 eggs, beaten**
- **4 tablespoons oil, plus extra for greasing**
- **300 g (10 oz) cooked rice**
- **525 g (17 oz) can creamed sweetcorn**
- **50 g (2 oz) onion, finely chopped**
- **2 tablespoons deseeded and finely chopped jalapeño or other chilli**
- **250 g (8 oz) Cheddar cheese, grated**

1 Sift the cornmeal, salt and bicarbonate of soda into a large mixing bowl. Add the milk, eggs, oil, rice, corn, onion, chilli and cheese, stirring only to blend well. Pour into a 30 cm (12 inch) cake tin or ovenproof frying pan which has been greased and sprinkled with cornmeal.

2 Cook the bread in a preheated oven, 180°C (350°F), Gas Mark 4, for 40–45 minutes.

Serves 8–10 / **Preparation time** 20 minutes / **Cooking time** 40–45 minutes

Serves 4 / **Preparation time** 10 minutes / **Cooking time** 15 minutes

chicken, bean and avocado rolls

- **4 large crusty rolls**
- **French mustard**
- **250 g (8 oz) can refried beans or see page 63**
- **2 cold roast chicken breasts, thinly sliced**
- **1 avocado, stoned, peeled and thinly sliced**
- **2 limes, quartered**
- **soured cream**
- **salt and pepper**

1 Warm the rolls in a preheated oven, 180° C (350°F), Gas Mark 4, for about 15 minutes.

2 Cut the rolls in half and spread the cut surfaces with mustard. Cover the bottom halves with refried beans, then cover with chicken slices, followed by avocado slices.

3 Sprinkle with salt and pepper, then squeeze over lime juice. Finish with soured cream to taste. Cover with the tops of the rolls and press together.

Serves 4 / **Preparation time** 10 minutes / **Cooking time** 20 minutes

ranchero eggs

- **2 garlic cloves**
- **2 green chillies, deseeded**
- **750 g (1½ lb) tomatoes, skinned and deseeded**
- **2 tablespoons vegetable oil, plus extra for cooking tortillas**
- **1 small onion, chopped**
- **½ teaspoon ground cumin**
- **8 x 10 cm (4 inch) tortillas or 4 x 20 cm (8 inch) tortillas**
- **8 eggs**
- **50 g (2 oz) Lancashire, Wensleydale or Cheshire cheese, finely crumbled**
- **salt**
- **chopped coriander, to garnish**

1 Finely chop the garlic and chillies in a food processor, then add the tomatoes and process until finely chopped, but not smooth.

2 Heat the 2 tablespoons of oil in a frying pan and fry the onion until soft. Add the cumin, tomato mixture and salt. Cook, stirring occasionally, until the sauce has thickened. Keep warm.

3 Meanwhile, heat a shallow layer of oil in a deep frying pan. Add the tortillas, 1 at a time, and cook until limp and blistered, turning once. Drain on kitchen paper and keep warm in a low oven.

4 Pour most of the oil from the pan and fry the eggs in batches for 2–3 minutes each, until the whites are set. Drain on kitchen paper. Alternatively poach the eggs until just set.

5 Put 2 small tortillas or 1 large tortilla on each plate and add 1 or 2 eggs to each one. Top with the sauce and scatter over the cheese. Garnish with chopped coriander.

eggs with prawns

- **knob of butter**
- **1 small onion, finely chopped**
- **2 garlic cloves, crushed and finely chopped**
- **1 large tomato, skinned, deseeded and finely chopped**
- **pinch of chilli flakes**
- **4 eggs, lightly beaten**
- **150 g (5 oz) cooked peeled prawns**
- **salt and pepper**
- **lime quarters, to serve**

1 Heat the butter in a frying pan. Add the onion and garlic and fry, stirring occasionally, until the onion is soft but not coloured.

2 Add the tomato and chilli flakes and cook for about 5 minutes.

3 Stir in the eggs with salt and pepper to taste. Stir gently with a wooden spoon over a low heat until the eggs are lightly scrambled and creamy. Stir in the prawns and cook for a further minute without stirring. Cut into wedges and serve, accompanied by lime quarters.

Serves 2 / **Preparation time** 5 minutes / **Cooking time** 10 minutes

scrambled eggs with tortilla strips

- 2 x 20 cm (8 inch) tortillas
- vegetable oil, for frying
- knob of butter
- 2 garlic cloves, chopped
- 1 red pepper, roasted, skinned, deseeded and sliced
- pinch of chilli flakes
- 1 teaspoon ground cumin
- 500 g (1 lb) tomatoes, skinned and chopped
- 5 eggs, lightly beaten
- 2 tablespoons chopped coriander leaves
- 3 spring onions, thinly sliced
- salt and pepper
- Salsa (see page 77), to serve

1 Cut the tortillas into 2.5 cm (1 inch) strips and fry in oil until crisp. Drain on kitchen paper.

2 Heat the butter in a frying pan. Add the garlic and red pepper and cook over a low heat for 1 minute. Stir in the chilli flakes and cumin, stir for about 30 seconds, then add the tomatoes. Cook for a further minute.

3 Season the eggs with salt and pepper and pour into the pan. Cook, stirring over a low heat, until the eggs are beginning to set. Stir in the tortilla strips and cook until the eggs are done to the desired degree and the strips are still slightly crisp.

4 Sprinkle over the coriander and spring onions and serve with salsa.

Serves 2 / **Preparation time** 10 minutes / **Cooking time** 10 minutes

cauliflower salad

- 1 cauliflower, divided into florets
- 1 recipe quantity Guacamole (see page 76)
- 1 tomato, skinned, deseeded and chopped
- 3 tablespoons olive oil
- 1 tablespoon white wine vinegar
- salt and pepper

TO SERVE
- crisp lettuce leaves
- freshly grated Parmesan cheese

1 Cook the cauliflower in boiling salted water until just tender. Drain well and rinse under cold running water.

2 Meanwhile, make the guacamole. Stir in the tomato.

3 Whisk together the oil and vinegar with salt and pepper to taste. Pour over the cauliflower and toss together. Leave until cold.

4 Put the lettuce in a shallow dish and add the cauliflower. Pour over the guacamole and sprinkle with grated Parmesan cheese.

Serves 6 / **Preparation time** 15 minutes / **Cooking time** 10 minutes

Serves 4 / **Preparation time** 15 minutes / **Cooking time** 15–20 minutes

vegetable fajitas

1 Heat the oil in a large frying pan and gently sauté the onions and garlic for about 5 minutes, until they are soft and golden brown.

2 Add the red and green peppers, chillies and oregano and stir well. Sauté gently for about 10 minutes, until cooked and tender.

3 Add the button mushrooms and cook quickly for 1 minute more, stirring to mix the mushrooms thoroughly with the other vegetables. Season the vegetable mixture with salt and pepper to taste.

4 To serve, spoon the sizzling hot vegetable mixture into the warmed tortillas and roll up or fold over. Serve hot, garnished with snipped chives.

- **2 tablespoons oil**
- **2 large onions, thinly sliced**
- **2 garlic cloves, crushed**
- **2 red peppers, deseeded and thinly sliced**
- **2 green peppers, deseeded and thinly sliced**
- **4 green chillies, deseeded and thinly sliced**
- **2 teaspoons chopped oregano**
- **250 g (8 oz) button mushrooms, sliced**
- **salt and pepper**
- **12 warmed tortillas, to serve**
- **snipped chives, to garnish**

Serves 6 / **Preparation time** 10 minutes, plus draining /
Cooking time 40 minutes

stuffed courgettes

- **6 large courgettes, about 750 g (1½ lb)**
- **275 g (9 oz) frozen sweetcorn kernels, thawed**
- **2 garlic cloves, crushed**
- **2 eggs**
- **2 tablespoons milk**
- **175 g (6 oz) feta cheese, rinsed and finely crumbled**
- **25 g (1 oz) butter, melted**
- **salt and pepper**

1 Halve the courgettes lengthways. Using a teaspoon, carefully scoop out the flesh to leave a 1 cm (½ inch) shell. Sprinkle salt inside the courgettes and leave upside down on a rack to drain for 1 hour.

2 Carefully but thoroughly wipe the insides of the courgettes to remove the salt. Put into a shallow ovenproof dish. Preheat the oven to 180°C (350°F), Gas Mark 4.

3 Process the sweetcorn, garlic, eggs, milk and pepper to a coarse purée in a food processor. Add 125 g (4 oz) of the feta cheese. Divide among the courgette shells. Scatter over the remaining cheese and trickle over the butter. Bake in the preheated oven for 30–40 minutes, until the courgettes are tender and the tops lightly browned; cover with foil if they brown too quickly.

quesadillas

- **12 tortillas**
- **175 g (6 oz) canned refried beans or see page 63**
- **375 g (12 oz) mixed Cheddar cheese, grated, and Mozzarella cheese, cut into strips**
- **4-6 green chillies, deseeded and thinly sliced**
- **oil, for frying**

TO SERVE
- **Salsa (see page 77)**
- **Guacamole (see page 76)**
- **soured cream**

1   Put the tortillas on a board and divide the refried bean mixture between them, putting a spoonful of mixture on one half of each tortilla, leaving a little space around the edge.

2   Put a little cheese on top of the beans and then add a few slices of chilli. Fold the tortilla over the top of the filling.

3   Press the edges of each folded tortilla firmly between your fingertips. It helps if the tortillas are soft and quite damp when you do this. If necessary, secure them with cocktail sticks. Cover the folded tortillas with a clean damp tea towel while you are making the remaining quesadillas.

4   Pour some oil in a large pan to a depth of 4 cm (1½ inches) and heat. Fry the quesadillas, in batches, until crisp and golden brown. Remove and drain on kitchen paper. Serve hot with salsa, guacamole and soured cream.

Serves 4–6 / **Preparation time** 15 minutes / **Cooking time** 5–10 minutes

empañadas

1 Mix the flour, salt and paprika in a bowl. Heat the butter, 1 tablespoon oil and water in a pan until the butter has melted. Stir into the flour and mix to a soft dough. Turn the dough out on to a lightly floured surface and knead briefly. Wrap in clingfilm and set aside to stand at room temperature for 30 minutes.

2 Place all the filling ingredients in a bowl and mix well. Roll out the pastry thinly on a lightly floured surface. Cut into 12 x 10 cm (4 inch) rounds with a pastry cutter. Put 2 teaspoons of filling on each round. Brush the pastry edges with water and fold each round in half. Pinch the edges to seal.

3 Pour oil to a depth of about 2.5 cm (1 inch) into a large frying pan. Heat the oil and fry the empañadas, a few at a time, for about 5 minutes, turning once, until evenly browned. Remove them from the hot oil with a slotted spoon and drain on kitchen paper. Serve the empañadas hot.

PASTRY
- **250 g (8 oz) plain flour**
- **½ teaspoon salt**
- **1 teaspoon paprika**
- **50 g (2 oz) butter**
- **1 tablespoon oil**
- **125 ml (4 fl oz) water**
- **oil, for deep-frying**

FILLING
- **2 spring onions, chopped**
- **1 tomato, skinned, deseeded and chopped**
- **50 g (2 oz) cooked ham, chopped**
- **50 g (2 oz) Cheddar cheese, grated**
- **200 g (7 oz) can creamed sweetcorn**
- **1 teaspoon chilli sauce**
- **salt and pepper**

Makes 12 / **Preparation time** 20 minutes, plus standing / **Cooking time** 12–15 minutes

meat-stuffed
tortillas with salsa

- **500 g (1 lb) minced pork**
- **500 g (1 lb) minced beef**
- **1 tablespoon oil**
- **1 large onion, finely chopped**
- **2 garlic cloves, crushed**
- **1 tablespoon chilli powder**
- **½ teaspoon ground cumin**
- **2 teaspoons dried oregano**
- **pinch of salt**
- **50 ml (2 fl oz) vinegar**
- **250 ml (8 fl oz) beef stock**
- **450 ml (¾ pint) Salsa (see page 77)**
- **12 tortillas**
- **75 g (3 oz) Cheddar cheese, grated**

TO GARNISH
- **sliced radishes or olives**
- **dried chilli flakes**
- **1 red chilli, deseeded and thinly sliced**

1 Put the minced pork and beef in a frying pan and cook in their own fat until browned and crumbly, breaking up the meat with a spoon. Add the oil, onion and garlic and cook until soft. Stir in the chilli powder, cumin, oregano and salt, then the vinegar and stock. Simmer for about 10 minutes, or until the liquid has evaporated. Remove from the heat and cool.

2 Spread some of the salsa over each tortilla and put about 2 tablespoons of the meat filling down the centre of each one. Fold over, secure with a cocktail stick and arrange in an ovenproof dish.

3 Pour the remaining salsa over the tortillas and sprinkle them with the grated Cheddar. Bake in a preheated oven, 180°C (350°F), Gas Mark 4, for 20-30 minutes until golden brown. Remove the tortillas from the dish and garnish with the radish or olive slices, chilli flakes and red chilli slices.

Serves 4 / **Preparation time** 20 minutes / **Cooking time** 30-40 minutes

Serves 4 / **Preparation time** 20 minutes / **Cooking time** 25–30 minutes

fried beef tortillas

- oil, for frying
- 8 tortillas
- 500 g (1 lb) minced beef
- 2 red chillies, deseeded and chopped
- 2 garlic cloves, crushed
- ½ teaspoon ground cumin
- 125 ml (4 fl oz) tomato purée
- 175 ml (6 fl oz) beef stock
- 1 tablespoon vinegar
- 2 tomatoes, skinned, deseeded and chopped
- red and green chillies, deseeded and chopped, to garnish

1 Heat about 5 mm (¼ inch) of oil in a large frying pan and fry the tortillas until they are crisp and golden – about 1 minute on each side. Set aside to keep warm while making the topping.

2 Put the minced beef in a clean frying pan and fry it gently in its own fat until it is cooked and browned, breaking it up as it cooks. Pour off and discard any excess fat.

3 Add the chillies, garlic, cumin, tomato purée, beef stock and vinegar. Bring to the boil, stirring constantly, and add the tomatoes. Reduce the heat and cook gently for 10–15 minutes, until reduced and thickened.

4 Put a large spoonful of the meat mixture on each fried tortilla. Serve garnished with red and green chillies.

Tip Called tostadas in Mexico, these are made by frying both the tortillas and the topping. You may prefer to fry the tortillas while the beef topping is cooking to ensure the tortillas are freshly made.

Serves 4 / **Preparation time** 15 minutes, plus marinating /
Cooking time 15 minutes

marinated
chicken kebabs

- **6 boneless chicken breasts**

MARINADE
- **juice of 2 limes**
- **1 tablespoon honey**
- **1 green chilli, deseeded and finely chopped**
- **2 tablespoons oil**

AVOCADO SAUCE
- **3 tablespoons oil**
- **1 tablespoon red wine vinegar**
- **1 large avocado, peeled, stoned and mashed**
- **1 large tomato, skinned, deseeded and chopped**
- **2 spring onions, chopped**
- **125 ml (4 fl oz) soured cream**

TO GARNISH
- **lime rind strips**
- **chilli flowers (see below)**

1 To make the marinade, pour the lime juice into a large bowl, add the honey, chilli and oil and mix until it is well blended and smooth.

2 Skin the chicken breasts and cut the flesh into long strips. Add the strips to the marinade and stir gently until well coated. Cover and chill for at least 1 hour.

3 Thread the chicken on to wooden skewers and brush with the marinade. Cook under a preheated hot grill or on a barbecue, turning occasionally, until the chicken is tender and golden brown. Brush the kebabs with more marinade, if necessary, while cooking.

4 Meanwhile, make the avocado sauce. Blend the oil and vinegar in a bowl, then beat in the mashed avocado until the mixture is thick and smooth. Stir in the chopped tomato and spring onions, then the soured cream. Garnish the sauce with strips of lime rind. Garnish the kebabs with chilli flowers and serve the kebabs with some avocado sauce.

Tip Make an elegant garnish for this dish by slicing a thin red chilli from its tip to the base of the stem several times (remove the seeds). The chilli will look rather like a flower if the strips are spread out.

Serves 4 / **Preparation time** 10 minutes / **Cooking time** 1 hour

chicken enchiladas

- **2 tablespoons oil**
- **2 red onions, sliced**
- **2 red peppers, deseeded and thinly sliced**
- **3 garlic cloves, crushed**
- **2 red chillies, deseeded and thinly sliced**
- **2 teaspoons ground cumin**
- **2 teaspoons ground coriander**
- **4 chicken breast fillets, cut into strips**
- **250 g (8 oz) can refried beans or see page 63**
- **300 ml (½ pint) soured cream**
- **4 tablespoons chopped coriander**
- **8 tortillas**
- **125 g (4 oz) mixed Cheddar and Mozzarella cheese, grated**
- **salt and pepper**

1 Heat the oil in a large pan. Add the onions, peppers, garlic and three-quarters of the chillies. Fry until softened and lightly coloured. Stir in the cumin and ground coriander, then the chicken strips. Cover and cook for 5 minutes.

2 Stir in the beans, 2 tablespoons of soured cream and three-quarters of the fresh coriander. Season to taste and set aside.

3 Place the tortillas on a work surface. Divide the chicken mixture between them, then roll up the tortillas and transfer them to a large, shallow ovenproof dish.

4 Spoon over the remaining soured cream and scatter over the grated cheese. Cover with foil and bake in a preheated oven, 190°C (375°F), Gas Mark 5, for 50 minutes, removing the foil and adding the remaining chillies and coriander 10 minutes before the end.

more than a mouthful

stuffed avocados

- 2 tablespoons oil
- 1 teaspoon wine vinegar
- juice of ½ lime
- 2 avocados
- salt and pepper

STUFFING

- 3 tablespoons oil
- 1 onion, finely chopped
- 1 garlic clove, crushed
- 125 g (4 oz) mushrooms, chopped
- 1 red chilli, deseeded and finely chopped
- 1 tablespoon chopped parsley
- rind of 1 lime, cut into fine strips, to serve

Variation

Soured Cream and Coriander Avocados

Replace the parsley in the stuffing with the same quantity of chopped coriander. Top the cooked avocados with soured cream and serve with warm tortillas.

1 To make the dressing, blend the oil with the wine vinegar and lime juice in a small bowl until thoroughly combined. Season with a little salt and pepper.

2 Cut the avocados in half and remove the pits. Brush the inner surfaces of the avocado halves with the lime dressing; this will add flavour and prevent the flesh from discolouring. Set the avocados aside while you prepare the stuffing.

3 Heat the oil in a heavy-based frying pan and sauté the onion and garlic over a low heat until soft and golden. Add the chopped mushrooms and chilli, and continue cooking for a few minutes, stirring occasionally, until cooked and golden brown. Stir in half the parsley.

4 Remove the stuffing mixture from the heat and pile it into the prepared avocado halves. Place them on a lightly oiled baking tray and warm them through in a preheated oven, 160°C (325°F), Gas Mark 3, for 10–15 minutes. Serve sprinkled with the remaining parsley and the strips of lime rind.

Serves 4 / **Preparation time** 25 minutes / **Cooking time** 10–15 minutes

Serves 4 / **Preparation time** 20 minutes / **Cooking time** 10 minutes

tortilla flutes

- **400 g (13 oz) canned refried beans or see page 63**
- **2 green chillies, deseeded and chopped**
- **50 g (2 oz) onion, chopped**
- **25 g (1 oz) toasted chopped almonds**
- **2 tablespoons chopped coriander**
- **125 g (4 oz) Cheddar cheese, grated**
- **8 tortillas**
- **oil, for deep-frying**

TO SERVE
- **Red Chilli Sauce (see page 77)**
- **1 avocado, stoned, peeled and sliced**

1 Put the refried beans and chillies in a pan and heat through gently, stirring occasionally so that they do not stick. Mix in the onion, almonds, coriander and cheese.

2 Meanwhile, wrap up the tortillas in foil and warm in a low oven to soften them. Spoon a little of the refried bean and cheese mixture along the centre of each warmed tortilla.

3 Roll up each tortilla carefully and tightly to form a flute. If necessary, secure with wooden cocktail sticks to prevent them from opening during the frying process.

4 Pour oil to a depth of about 2.5 cm (1 inch) into a heavy-based frying pan and heat. Fry the flutes, in batches, until they are crisp and lightly browned all over. Drain on kitchen paper. Serve with red chilli sauce and avocado slices.

panuchos

- **2 onions, sliced**
- **5 tablespoons wine vinegar**
- **125 ml (4 fl oz) chicken stock**
- **½ teaspoon ground cumin**
- **½ teaspoon dried oregano**
- **1 garlic clove, crushed**
- **750 g (1½ lb) cooked chicken, thinly sliced**
- **12 corn tortillas, fried until puffed**
- **250 g (8 oz) can refried beans or see page 63**
- **4 hard-boiled eggs, sliced**
- **Red Chilli Sauce (see page 77)**

1 Place the onions, vinegar, stock, cumin, oregano and garlic in a pan. Cover and simmer for 5 minutes. Add the chicken and heat through. Drain if necessary.

2 Make a slit at the base of each puffed tortilla and open to make a cavity. Fill with about 3 tablespoons of the refried beans and a few egg slices. Top each panucho with about 2 tablespoons of the chicken mixture and spoon over some red chilli sauce.

Tip If the tortillas will not puff up, spread the beans on to the fried tortillas and top with the egg slices, chicken mixture and sauce.

chimichangas

- **2 tablespoons oil**
- **1 small onion, chopped**
- **1 red pepper, deseeded and chopped**
- **125 g (4 oz) button mushrooms, thinly sliced**
- **2 tomatoes, skinned, deseeded and chopped**
- **2 red chillies, deseeded and finely chopped**
- **175 g (6 oz) mixed Cheddar and Mozzarella cheese, grated**
- **8 tortillas**
- **oil, for deep-frying**
- **salt and pepper**
- **coriander sprigs, to serve**

TO GARNISH

- **skin of 2 courgettes, very thinly sliced into strips**
- **sea salt**

1   Heat the oil in a heavy-based frying pan. Add the onion and red pepper and sauté until just tender, but still slightly crisp. Add the mushrooms, tomatoes and chillies and stir-fry over a medium heat for 3–4 minutes. Season to taste with salt and pepper.

2   Remove the frying pan from the heat, and mix the grated cheese into the stir-fried vegetable mixture. Stir gently until the cheese melts.

3   Divide the vegetable and cheese mixture into 8 portions and put 1 in the centre of each tortilla. Carefully fold the two opposite sides of the tortillas over the filling, then fold the loose edges under so that the filling is completely sealed.

4   Heat sufficient oil for deep-frying in a heavy-based frying pan and fry the tortillas, 1 or 2 at a time, in the hot oil until crisp and golden, turning once during cooking. Remove from the oil with a slotted spoon and drain on kitchen paper, keeping the tortillas warm while frying the remaining batches. Serve on a bed of fresh coriander, garnished with courgette strips and sprinkled with sea salt.

Serves 4 / **Preparation time** 20 minutes / **Cooking time** 15–20 minutes

garlic prawns

- **24 raw king prawns**
- **6 garlic cloves**
- **salt and whole black peppercorns**
- **2 red chillies, deseeded and finely chopped**
- **3 tablespoons oil**
- **50 g (2 oz) butter**
- **juice of 2 limes**
- **3 tablespoons chopped coriander**

TO SERVE
- **lime wedges**
- **sliced avocado**
- **warm tortillas**

1 To prepare the prawns, remove the heads and, leaving them in their shells, split them carefully down the middle towards the tail end without completely separating them. They should look a little like butterflies. Remove the dark vein running along the back of the prawns.

2 Peel the garlic cloves and crush them with the salt, peppercorns and chopped chillies in a mortar with a pestle to a thick aromatic paste.

3 Coat the prepared prawns with the garlic paste and place them in a bowl. Scrape out any of the remaining garlic paste over the top, then cover the bowl and leave in a cool place to marinate for at least 1 hour.

4 Heat the oil and butter in a large heavy-based frying pan and add the prawns and garlic paste. Quickly sauté them over a medium heat for 2–3 minutes, until they turn pink. Remove from the pan and keep warm. Add the lime juice to the pan and stir into the pan juices. Boil vigorously for a couple of minutes and then pour over the prawns. Sprinkle with chopped coriander and serve with lime wedges, sliced avocado and warm tortillas.

Serves 4–6 / **Preparation time** 15 minutes, plus marinating / **Cooking time** 5 minutes

crab-stuffed tortillas

1 Butter an ovenproof dish large enough to take the rolled-up tortillas in one layer.

2 Heat the oil in a large frying pan and shallow-fry the tortillas, 1 at a time, over a moderate heat for a few seconds until they become limp. Take care not to overcook the tortillas; they must not be allowed to become crisp.

3 Pat the tortillas with absorbent kitchen paper to remove any excess oil. Spread each one with a little salsa.

4 Put some crabmeat on the middle of each tortilla. Sprinkle the cheese on top, reserving a little, then add some red onion. Roll up the tortillas and put them in the prepared dish.

5 Pour the remaining salsa over the top of the tortillas and sprinkle with the rest of the cheese. Bake in a preheated oven, 200°C (400°F), Gas Mark 6, for 15–20 minutes. Serve the tortillas with soured cream, snipped chives and chilli flakes.

- **butter, for greasing**
- **oil, for frying**
- **12 tortillas**
- **450 ml (¾ pint) Salsa (see page 77)**
- **500 g (1 lb) crabmeat**
- **350 g (12 oz) mixed Cheddar and mozzarella cheese, grated**
- **1 small red onion, finely chopped**

TO SERVE
- **soured cream**
- **snipped chives**
- **dried chilli flakes**

Tip Tortillas stuffed and baked in a sauce are called enchiladas on Mexican menus. The stuffing can be fish or shellfish, as here, meat, as in the Meat-stuffed Tortillas with Salsa (see page 37), or vegetables.

Serves 4–6 / **Preparation time** 15 minutes / **Cooking time** 20–25 minutes

Serves 5–6 / **Preparation time** 25 minutes, plus cooling and chilling / **Cooking time** 20–25 minutes

prawn empañadas

- **2 tablespoons oil**
- **1 large onion, finely chopped**
- **2 garlic cloves, crushed**
- **4 tablespoons tomato purée**
- **500 g (1 lb) cooked peeled prawns, chopped**
- **4 green chillies, deseeded and finely chopped**
- **1 teaspoon ground cumin**
- **1 teaspoon ground allspice**
- **2 teaspoons chopped oregano**
- **1 tablespoon lime juice**
- **20 tortillas**
- **oil, for deep-frying**
- **salt and pepper**
- **soured cream, to serve**
- **chopped coriander, to garnish**

1   Heat the oil in a heavy-based frying pan, add the onion and garlic and sauté over a low heat until soft and golden. Stir in the tomato purée, prawns, chillies, cumin, allspice, oregano, lime juice and salt and pepper to taste. Cook gently until the mixture reduces and thickens a little, then set aside to cool.

2   Put a small spoonful of the cooled prawn mixture in the centre of each tortilla. Fold the dough over the prawn filling, then dampen and press the edges together firmly between your fingers to seal them. Repeat in this way until all the empañadas are sealed.

3   Cover the empañadas with clingfilm and chill in the refrigerator until you are ready to cook and serve them.

4   Heat sufficient oil for deep-frying in a large saucepan. Put the empañadas, in small batches, into the oil and fry until golden. Drain on absorbent kitchen paper and keep warm. Serve the empañadas hot, with soured cream and garnished with coriander.

Serves 4 / **Preparation time** 20 minutes / **Cooking time** 1½ hours

burritos with pork stuffing

- 1 kg (2 lb) boneless rolled pork shoulder
- 1 tablespoon oil
- 350 ml (12 fl oz) meat stock
- 250 ml (8 fl oz) passata
- ½ teaspoon grated orange rind
- 1 teaspoon dried chilli flakes, plus extra to garnish
- 8 tortillas
- salt
- soured cream, to serve
- ½ avocado, stoned, peeled and finely sliced, to garnish

1 Put the pork shoulder in a roasting tin and brush with a little of the oil. Sprinkle with salt, transfer to a preheated oven, 180°C (350°F), Gas Mark 4, and cook for about 1½ hours, or until crisp, golden and cooked through.

2 Meanwhile, make the sauce. Put the meat stock into a small saucepan with the passata, orange rind and most of the dried chilli flakes. Bring to the boil, reduce the heat and simmer gently for about 30 minutes, until the sauce is reduced and thickened.

3 Remove any fat from the cooked pork and tear the meat into shreds, using a fork. Add to the sauce and heat through very gently over a low heat.

4 Wrap the tortillas in foil and heat through gently in a moderate oven. Place a little of the pork mixture in the centre of each tortilla and roll them up. Serve the burritos with soured cream, garnished with avocado slices and the extra chilli flakes.

mexican stuffed peppers

- **6 large green peppers**
- **1 recipe quantity Savoury Minced Beef (see page 71)**
- **2 eggs, separated**
- **flour, for coating**
- **oil, for frying**
- **salt and pepper**
- **1 quantity Salsa (see page 77), to serve**

1 Make a long split in the side of each pepper and carefully scoop out the seeds without tearing the pepper. Trim the stalks if they are long. Stuff each pepper with about one-sixth of the savoury minced beef mixture.

2 Beat the egg whites in a bowl until they form stiff peaks. In a separate bowl, beat the egg yolks with salt and pepper until lightly coloured, then gently fold in the beaten egg white.

3 Dip the stuffed peppers in the flour and then into the egg mixture. Pour the oil into a heavy-based frying pan to a depth of 1 cm (½ inch) and heat. Fry the peppers, in batches, over a low heat, turning occasionally, until they are uniformly golden all over and the filling is sealed inside the egg coating. Drain on kitchen paper.

4 Serve the peppers, cut into slices, with a little salsa.

Serves 6 / **Preparation time** 25 minutes / **Cooking time** 15–20 minutes

Serves 4 / **Preparation time** 20–25 minutes /
Cooking time about 30 minutes

beef tacos

1 Put the minced beef in a frying pan
and fry it gently in its own fat until it is
cooked and browned, breaking it up
as it cooks. Pour off and discard any
excess fat. Add the onion, pepper and
garlic and cook, stirring occasionally,
until softened. Stir in the oregano,
spices and salt and pepper to taste,
then add the tomato purée and mix
well. Cover and cook gently for 10
minutes, stirring occasionally.

2 Meanwhile, heat the taco shells in a
preheated oven, 180°C (350°F), Gas
Mark 4. Serve the beef filling in the
hot taco shells accompanied by
shredded red cabbage and soured
cream, and garnish with paprika.

- **500 g (1 lb) minced beef**
- **75 g (3 oz) onion,
  finely chopped**
- **65 g (2½ oz) green pepper,
  deseeded and finely chopped**
- **1 garlic clove, crushed**
- **1 teaspoon dried oregano**
- **½ teaspoon hot paprika, plus
  extra to garnish**
- **¼ teaspoon ground cumin**
- **¼ teaspoon dried hot red
  pepper flakes**
- **125 ml (4 fl oz) tomato purée**
- **12 taco shells**
- **salt and pepper**

TO SERVE
- **shredded red cabbage**
- **soured cream**

chicken-filled tortillas

- **6 chicken breast fillets, skinned and cut into small pieces**
- **2 tablespoons oil**
- **2 large onions, sliced**
- **1 red pepper, cored, deseeded and cut into strips**
- **1 green pepper, cored, deseeded and cut into strips**
- **12 soft tortillas, warmed**
- **250 g (8 oz) Guacamole (see page 76)**
- **300 ml (½ pint) soured cream**
- **2 tablespoons toasted sesame seeds**
- **1 tablespoon chopped coriander**

MARINADE

- **juice of 4 limes**
- **3 tablespoons oil**
- **1 teaspoon dried oregano**
- **1 teaspoon dried coriander**

1 Make the marinade: combine all the ingredients in a bowl. Add the chicken, cover and chill for 4 hours.

2 Put the chicken and marinade in a roasting tin, cover with foil and bake in a preheated oven, 200°C (400°F), Gas Mark 6, for 30 minutes. Remove the foil for the last 10 minutes.

3 Heat the oil in a frying pan and sauté the onions and the red and green peppers. Place a little of the mixture on each tortilla, and top with chicken, guacamole, soured cream and sesame seeds. Sprinkle with chopped coriander and roll up the tortillas into cone shapes.

Serves 4 / **Preparation time** 30 minutes, plus chilling / **Cooking time** 40 minutes

little meals

spicy chickpeas

refried beans

green rice

mexican salad

christmas eve salad

ceviche

acapulco-style prawns

'dry' soup with pasta

savoury minced beef

meatballs with tomato sauce

spiced pork steaks

Serves 4 / **Preparation time** 30 minutes, plus soaking / **Cooking time** about 2 hours

spicy chickpeas

- **300 g (10 oz) dried chickpeas**
- **1½ teaspoons salt**
- **1 whole onion, peeled**
- **6 streaky bacon rashers, chopped**
- **2 onions, chopped**
- **1 garlic clove, crushed**
- **1 red pepper, deseeded and chopped**
- **¼ teaspoon ground black pepper**
- **1 small dried hot red chilli, crumbled**
- **½ teaspoon dried oregano**
- **300 g (10 oz) tomatoes, skinned and chopped**
- **2 tablespoons tomato purée**
- **6 tablespoons water or reserved chickpea liquid**
- **2 tablespoons chopped coriander**

1   Soak the chickpeas overnight in cold water. Drain and place in a saucepan with 1 teaspoon of the salt and the whole onion. Cover with cold water.

2   Bring to the boil, then reduce the heat and simmer, uncovered, for at least 1½ hours or until the chickpeas are cooked and tender. Drain the chickpeas, reserving the cooking liquid. Discard the onion.

3   Put the bacon in a frying pan and fry until the fat starts to run. Add the chopped onions, garlic and red pepper and continue frying until soft. Stir in the remaining salt, the pepper, chilli, oregano, tomatoes, tomato purée and some of the reserved chickpea cooking liquid.

4   Add the drained chickpeas and stir well. Simmer for 10 minutes, stirring occasionally. Serve hot, sprinkled with chopped coriander leaves.

refried beans

- 250 g (8 oz) dried pinto beans
- 4 garlic cloves, crushed
- 1 bay leaf
- 4 tablespoons bacon fat or oil
- 175 g (6 oz) chopped onion
- 50 g (2 oz) Monterey Jack or Cheddar cheese, grated
- salt and pepper

TO GARNISH
- Guacamole (see page 76)
- soured cream
- avocado slices
- Salsa (see page 77)

1   Put the beans in a large bowl and cover with cold water. Leave to soak for at least 6 hours or, preferably, overnight. The following day, drain the beans and rinse them well under cold running water.

2   Put the beans in a large saucepan with the garlic and bay leaf. Cover with cold water and bring to the boil. Boil briskly for 10 minutes, then lower the heat to a bare simmer and cook gently for about 2 hours, until the beans are very tender.

3   Drain the beans, reserving the cooking liquid. Discard the bay leaf. Mash the beans coarsely with a potato masher or process in a food processor or blender, adding some of the reserved liquid as necessary until you achieve the desired consistency.

4   Melt the bacon fat in a frying pan or heat the oil and sauté the onion, stirring, until soft. Add the beans and salt and pepper to taste and mix well. Simmer until hot, continuing to mash and add more liquid as necessary. Serve hot, sprinkled with cheese, garnished with guacamole, soured cream, avocado slices and salsa.

Serves 4–6 / **Preparation time** 20 minutes, plus soaking / **Cooking time** 2¼ hours

green rice

1 Heat 3 tablespoons of the oil in a
   heavy-based frying pan and stir in the
   rice. Cook, stirring frequently, until all
   the grains of rice are coated with oil
   and glistening.

2 Add the onion, garlic and tomatoes,
   and cook for 2 minutes. Add about
   350 ml (12 fl oz) of the stock, cover
   the pan and simmer gently for about
   25 minutes, or until the rice is tender
   and has absorbed all the liquid. Keep
   checking the rice and adding more
   stock as necessary. Season to taste
   with salt and pepper.

3 Five minutes before the end of the
   cooking time, heat the remaining oil
   in another frying pan and stir-fry the
   pepper strips until they start to lose
   their crispness, but still retain their
   bright green colour.

4 Add the pepper strips and olive slices
   to the cooked rice and serve.

- **5 tablespoons oil**
- **175 g (6 oz) long grain rice**
- **1 onion, finely chopped**
- **1 garlic clove, crushed**
- **400 g (13 oz) can chopped tomatoes, drained**
- **450 ml (¾ pint) vegetable stock**
- **2 green peppers, cored, deseeded and cut into thin strips**
- **125 g (4 oz) pimiento-stuffed green olives, sliced**
- **salt and pepper**

Serves 4 / **Preparation time** 10 minutes / **Cooking time** 30 minutes

Serves 4 / **Preparation time** 15 minutes / **Cooking time** 15 minutes

mexican salad

- **400 g (13 oz) can red kidney beans**
- **4 tablespoons oil**
- **4 tortillas**
- **125 g (4 oz) lettuce, shredded**
- **4 slices cooked ham, cut into strips**
- **125 g (4 oz) cheese, cut into strips**

TOPOPO DRESSING

- **150 ml (¼ pint) oil**
- **5 tablespoons vinegar**
- **1 teaspoon salt**
- **½ teaspoon brown sugar**
- **½ teaspoon paprika**
- **½ teaspoon dry mustard**
- **¼ teaspoon pepper**
- **⅛ teaspoon Tabasco sauce**

TO GARNISH

- **black olives**
- **red and green chillies, deseeded and chopped**
- **cherry tomatoes**

1 Coarsely mash the beans with their liquid in a frying pan. Stir in 2 tablespoons of the oil. Cook for about 10 minutes over a medium heat, stirring to prevent sticking, until all the liquid is absorbed; set aside. Heat the remaining oil in a second frying pan, add the tortillas and fry over a medium heat until lightly browned on both sides. Drain on kitchen paper.

2 Place all the ingredients for the dressing in a screw-top jar and shake well. Chill.

3 Spread the tortillas generously with the beans. Pile the lettuce on top. Arrange alternate strips of ham and cheese over the lettuce. Garnish with olives, chillies and tomatoes and serve with the chilled dressing.

christmas eve salad

- **1 green apple, cored and sliced**
- **2 oranges, segmented**
- **½ fresh pineapple, peeled, cored and sliced**
- **1 large banana, sliced**
- **1 large red apple, cored and sliced**
- **125 ml (4 fl oz) lime juice**
- **1 large lettuce, separated into leaves**
- **2 small cooked beetroots, peeled and diced**

DRESSING

- **6 tablespoons oil**
- **2 tablespoons lime juice**
- **1 teaspoon sugar**
- **¼ teaspoon salt**

TO GARNISH

- **75 g (3 oz) unsalted roasted peanuts**
- **1 tablespoon chopped coriander**

1 Prepare all the fruit and sprinkle with lime juice to prevent discoloration.

2 To make the dressing, mix all the ingredients together and blend thoroughly or put into a screw-top jar and shake vigorously until the sugar has completely dissolved.

3 Arrange the lettuce, beetroot and fruit on a plate and sprinkle the dressing over the top of the salad.

4 Garnish the salad with the peanuts and coriander and serve immediately.

Serves 4–6 / **Preparation time** 25 minutes

Serves 4 / **Preparation time** 15 minutes, plus marinating

ceviche

- **500 g (1 lb) mixed seafood, such as fillets of sole, flounder, haddock, scallops and prawns**
- **125 ml (4 fl oz) lime juice**
- **2 tomatoes, skinned, deseeded and chopped**
- **½ teaspoon dried red chilli flakes**
- **1 tablespoon oil**
- **½ teaspoon salt**
- **pinch of dried oregano**
- **pepper**
- **2 limes, cut into wedges, to garnish**

1 Clean the fish, rinse in cold water, and pat dry with kitchen paper. Cut the fish and scallops into thin slices. Peel the prawns, removing the black vein that runs along the back.

2 Put all the fish in a ceramic bowl and pour the lime juice over the top, making sure all the fish is well coated in the juice. Cover and chill in the refrigerator for 3–4 hours, or until the fish has become opaque.

3 Stir the tomatoes, chilli flakes, oil, salt, oregano and pepper into the chilled fish. Mix well and chill for another 2–3 hours. Leave to stand at room temperature for 15 minutes before serving, then garnish with lime wedges.

Tip This delicious method of preparing seafood is used throughout Latin America. The acidity of the lime juice in the marinade 'cooks' the fish, which is ready when it has become opaque. Choose seafood that is as fresh as possible.

acapulco-style prawns

- **500 g (1 lb) large raw prawns**
- **300 ml (½ pint) water**
- **25 g (1 oz) butter**
- **½ onion, finely chopped**
- **3 garlic cloves, crushed**
- **1 green chilli, deseeded and finely chopped**
- **3 tablespoons chopped parsley**
- **3 large tomatoes, skinned and chopped**
- **2 tablespoons tomato purée**
- **juice of 1 lime**
- **salt and pepper**

TO GARNISH
- **2 tablespoons chopped parsley**
- **lime wedges**
- **boiled rice, to serve**

1 Peel the prawns, removing the black vein that runs along the back. Put them aside while you bring the shells and water to the boil in a small pan. Simmer gently for 15–20 minutes, and then strain into a clean jug, discarding the shells.

2 Heat the butter in a large heavy-based frying pan and sauté the onion and garlic until soft and golden. Add the chilli and parsley, and sauté, stirring, for about 2 minutes, until the parsley turns dark green.

3 Add the tomatoes, tomato purée and lime juice. Season to taste with salt and pepper, and simmer for about 10–15 minutes, until the mixture thickens and reduces.

4 Add the reserved prawn stock and simmer for 5 minutes, stirring occasionally. Gently stir in the peeled prawns and cook for a further 2–3 minutes, until they turn pink. Serve on a bed of rice, garnished with chopped parsley and lime wedges.

Serves 4 / **Preparation time** 30 minutes / **Cooking time** 20–25 minutes

'dry' soup with pasta

- **2 tablespoons oil**
- **1 large onion, chopped**
- **3 garlic cloves, crushed and chopped**
- **175 g (6 oz) piece of chorizo sausage, skinned and finely chopped**
- **1 red pepper, cored, deseeded and chopped**
- **175 g (6 oz) angel hair pasta or vermicelli, broken into lengths**
- **2 x 400 g (13 oz) cans chopped tomatoes**
- **600 ml (1 pint) chicken stock**
- **½ teaspoon dried oregano**
- **salt**

TO SERVE
- **freshly grated Parmesan cheese**
- **green chillies, deseeded and chopped**

1 Heat the oil in a pan, add the onion, garlic and chorizo and fry until the vegetables have softened and browned. Stir in the red pepper and cook until softened.

2 Stir in the angel hair pasta or vermicelli. Add the tomatoes, stock and oregano, bring to the boil, then lower the heat and boil gently, uncovered, until the pasta is tender and the liquid is reduced to a sauce-like consistency. Leave to stand for 10–15 minutes.

3 Reheat, season with salt and serve sprinkled with Parmesan and chillies.

Serves 4 / **Preparation time** 5 minutes, plus standing / **Cooking time** 30 minutes

Serves 4 / **Preparation time** 10 minutes / **Cooking time** 30 minutes

savoury minced beef

- 2 tablespoons oil
- 1 onion, finely chopped
- 3 garlic cloves, crushed
- 1 teaspoon ground cumin
- 1–2 red chillies, deseeded and finely chopped
- 125 g (4 oz) piece of chorizo sausage, skinned and finely chopped
- 350 g (12 oz) lean minced beef
- 300 ml (½ pint) veal or chicken stock
- 175 ml (6 fl oz) tomato passata
- 50 g (2 oz) pitted black olives, sliced
- salt

1 Heat the oil in a frying pan and cook the onion and garlic until softened. Add the cumin and chillies, stir for 1 minute, then stir in the chorizo and fry for 6–8 minutes, until browned.

2 Add the minced beef, breaking it up with a wooden spoon. Cook, stirring occasionally, until the colour has changed from pink to brown.

3 Stir in the stock and passata and heat until bubbling around the edges. Simmer gently until the surplus liquid has evaporated. Stir in the olives and season with salt.

Serves 4 / **Preparation time** 10 minutes, plus chilling / **Cooking time** 25 minutes

meatballs with tomato sauce

- **500 g (1lb) minced pork**
- **1 garlic clove, very finely chopped**
- **½ onion, finely chopped**
- **1½ teaspoons dried oregano**
- **1 egg, lightly beaten**
- **2 teaspoons lime juice**
- **salt and pepper**

TOMATO SAUCE

- **1 tablespoon oil**
- **1 small onion, finely chopped**
- **2 garlic cloves, crushed**
- **1 small red chilli, deseeded and finely chopped**
- **1 red pepper, deseeded and chopped**
- **400 g (13 oz) can chopped tomatoes**
- **1 tablespoon tomato purée**
- **chopped parsley, to garnish**

1 Mix together the pork, garlic, onion, oregano, beaten egg, lime juice and seasoning until paste-like. With wet hands, form into 20 small balls. Cover and chill for about 1 hour.

2 Meanwhile, make the sauce. Heat the oil, add the onion, garlic, chilli and red pepper, and cook until softened. Stir in the tomatoes and tomato purée. Bring to the boil, cover and simmer for 10 minutes.

3 Cook the meatballs under a preheated hot grill for 8–10 minutes, turning frequently, until evenly browned. Serve with forks or cocktail sticks. Garnish the sauce with parsley and serve with the meatballs for dipping into.

spiced pork steaks

- 1 small onion, finely chopped
- 3 garlic cloves, crushed and finely chopped
- 2 teaspoons paprika
- 2 teaspoons chilli powder
- 1 teaspoon ground cumin
- 1 tablespoon oil
- 4 pork steaks
- chopped coriander
- salt

TO SERVE
- lime wedges
- avocado slices
- tomato slices

1 Using a pestle and mortar, pound the onion, garlic, paprika, chilli powder, cumin and oil.

2 Spread the spice mixture over both sides of the pork steaks. Place them individually between 2 pieces of clingfilm. Using a meat mallet or rolling pin, pound each steak until it is about 5 mm (¼ inch) thick.

3 Remove the clingfilm and cook the steaks under a preheated grill for about 2 minutes on each side, until cooked through.

4 Sprinkle the steaks with salt and coriander. Cut into strips and serve immediately with lime wedges and avocado and tomato slices.

Serves 4 / **Preparation time** 10 minutes / **Cooking time** 4 minutes

salsas and dips

guacamole

salsa

red chilli sauce

chilli bean dip

sausage dip

chilli cheese dip

Serves 4–6 / **Preparation time** 5 minutes, plus chilling /
Cooking time 5 minutes

guacamole

- **2 large ripe avocados**
- **3 tablespoons lime juice**
- **2 garlic cloves, crushed**
- **40 g (1½ oz) spring onions, chopped**
- **1–2 tablespoons deseeded and chopped green chillies**
- **125 g (4 oz) tomatoes, skinned, deseeded and chopped**
- **salt and pepper**
- **rind of 1 lime, cut into strips, to garnish**

TORTILLA CHIPS
- **8 tortillas**
- **oil, for deep-frying**
- **1 tablespoon paprika**

1   Cut the avocados in half and remove the pits. Using a spoon, scoop out the flesh into a bowl, add the lime juice and mash coarsely.

2   Add the garlic, spring onions and chillies, and season to taste. Mix in the chopped tomatoes. Cover and chill in the refrigerator for at least 1 hour.

3   Meanwhile, make the tortilla chips. Cut each tortilla into 8 equal pieces. Heat the oil to 180–190°C (350–375°F) or until a cube of bread browns in 30 seconds. Add the tortilla chips and deep-fry until crisp and golden. Drain on kitchen paper and sprinkle with a little paprika and salt. Serve the guacamole with the tortilla chips and garnish with strips of lime rind.

Tip To prevent the guacamole from discolouring, cover it tightly with clingfilm until ready to serve. Pushing the avocado pit into the centre of the guacamole also helps preserve its colour.

Serves 4–6 / **Preparation time** 10 minutes

salsa

- **6 small ripe tomatoes, skinned and finely chopped**
- **1–2 red or green chillies, deseeded and finely chopped**
- **2 tablespoons finely chopped onion**
- **2 tablespoons chopped coriander**
- **2 tablespoons lime juice**
- **2 teaspoons vinegar**
- **¼ teaspoon salt (optional)**
- **pepper**

1 Place all the ingredients in a food processor or blender and process until smooth.

red chilli sauce

- **5 small dried red chillies, crumbled**
- **3 tablespoons boiling water**
- **400 g (13 oz) can chopped tomatoes**
- **4 tablespoons oil**
- **2 onions, chopped**
- **2 garlic cloves, minced**
- **3 tablespoons tomato purée**
- **1 teaspoon ground cumin**
- **1 teaspoon ground coriander**
- **1½ tablespoons vinegar**
- **1 teaspoon sugar**

1 Place the chillies and boiling water in a food processor or blender. Drain the tomatoes, reserving the juice, and add the chopped tomatoes to the chillies. Blend until smooth, then pour into a jug. Heat the oil in a small frying pan and sauté the onions and garlic until soft. Stir in the blended tomato mixture, the reserved tomato juice, tomato purée, cumin, coriander, vinegar and sugar. Cover and simmer for 10 minutes.

Tip You can serve this sauce with tacos, enchiladas, meat, poultry and fish dishes.

Makes about 350 ml (12 fl oz) / **Preparation time** about 10 minutes / **Cooking time** 15 minutes

Serves 4 / **Preparation time** 15 minutes / **Cooking time** 30 minutes

chilli bean dip

- 2 large red peppers
- 2 tablespoons oil
- 2 garlic cloves, crushed
- 1 small red chilli, deseeded and finely chopped
- 400 g (13 oz) can red kidney beans, drained
- ½ teaspoon paprika
- dash of Tabasco sauce (optional)
- salt and pepper
- 2 tablespoons snipped chives, to garnish

Tip This spicy dip is excellent with crudités, tortilla chips or fingers of warm or toasted pitta bread.

1 Halve the peppers lengthways and remove the seeds. Lightly brush them inside and out with a little of the oil. Place on a lightly oiled baking sheet and roast in a preheated oven, 240°C (475°F), Gas Mark 9, for 15 minutes. Turn the peppers over and continue to roast until the edges begin to blacken and the flesh and skin begin to crumple. This will probably take another 15 minutes. Remove the peppers from the oven and leave until cool enough to handle, then peel off the skins.

2 Put the red pepper flesh, garlic and chilli in a blender or food processor and process until well chopped. Add the beans and paprika and continue to process until a coarse purée forms (this won't take long). Season with Tabasco, if using, and salt and pepper. With the machine running, add the rest of the oil to make a thick paste.

3 Pile the bean purée into a bowl and sprinkle with the chives. Cover and chill until ready to serve.

Serves 4 / **Preparation time** 20 minutes

sausage dip

- **1 avocado**
- **1 tablespoon lime juice**
- **¼ teaspoon dry mustard**
- **1 teaspoon Worcestershire sauce**
- **2 drops Tabasco sauce**
- **250 g (8 oz) chorizo sausage, skinned and finely chopped**
- **25 g (1 oz) onion, finely chopped**
- **1 tomato, skinned and chopped**

TO SERVE
- **vegetable sticks**
- **tortilla chips**

1 Halve and peel the avocado and remove and reserve the stone. Mash the avocado with the lime juice. Add the mustard, Worcestershire sauce and Tabasco sauce and mix well. Fold in the sausage, onion and tomato. Place the avocado stone in the centre of the mixture and chill.

2 Remove the avocado pit and serve the dip with vegetable sticks and tortilla chips.

chilli cheese dip

- **250 g (8 oz) Monterey Jack or mature Cheddar cheese, cubed**
- **250 ml (8 fl oz) soured cream**
- **2 green chillies, deseeded and diced**
- **½ garlic clove, crushed**
- **¼ teaspoon salt**

TO SERVE
- **carrot sticks**
- **celery sticks**
- **tortilla chips**

1 Place the cheese and soured cream in a blender and blend until smooth. Transfer to a bowl and stir in the chillies, garlic and salt. Check the consistency, adding more soured cream if necessary. Chill until required.

2 Serve with carrot and celery sticks and tortilla chips for dipping.

Serves 4–6 / **Preparation time** 20 minutes

acknowledgements

Picture credits
Octopus Publishing Group Ltd./Bill Reavell 6 left, 8 left, 15, 16, 66, 70, 73, /David Loftus 20, /Graham Kirk 6 right, 7 left, 23, 30, 46, 49, 62, 63, 69, 69 right, /Ian Wallace 14, 43, /Sandra Lane 9 centre, 25, 27, 31, 61, 78, /Sean Myers 1, 3, 4 left, 4 right, 5 left, 5 right, 6 centre, 7 centre, 8 right, 8 centre, 9 left, 9 right, 11, 13, 32, 35, 36, 37, 39, 40, 45, 50, 53, 54, 56, 59, 64, 68, 71, 75, 76

Editor: Abi Rowsell
Copy editor: Anne Lee
Proofreader: Linda Doeser
Indexer: Hilary Bird
Executive Art Editor: Geoff Fennell
Designer: Louise Griffiths
Production Controller: Jo Sim
Picture researcher: Jennifer Veall